Understanding Bitcoin Protocol

Understanding Bitcoin Protocol

Ultimate Guide to the World of Crypto currency, Bitcoin, Blockchain Technology, Exchanges and Trading strategies

From Beginner to Expert

Precious Godson

Copyright © 2018 Precious Godson

All rights reserved. Licensed for educational use only

Table of content

- Lesson One
  Bitcoin Basics
- Lesson Two
  Blockchain Technology
- Lesson Three
  Bitcoin Value
- Lesson Four
  How to Acquire Bitcoin
- Lesson Five
  Bitcoin Speculations
- Lesson Six
  Risks of Using Bitcoins
- Lesson Seven
  Bitcoin Wallets
- Lesson Eight
  Bitcoin Exchanges
- Lesson Nine
  Coinbase
- Lesson Ten
  How to Make Money Trading Bitcoin
- Lesson Eleven
  Bitcoin Trading Strategy

To my dearest friend Edafe

Disclaimer

Precious Godson is not a financial adviser, and nothing in this book is meant to be a recommendation to buy/sell any financial instrument.

I will never ask you to send me any amount of money in order to trade for you. Please report any suspicious emails or fake social media profiles claiming to be me.

Do not invest money you cannot afford to lose. There are no guarantees or certainties in trading. My books may contain list of websites and names of exchanges that I believe may add value to your life as a trader.

Make your own trading investments and decisions.

Lesson One
Bitcoin Basics

What is Bitcoin? Simply put, bitcoin is a decentralized digital currency. In other words, it is a kind of virtual cash or gold, and transferred person-to-person. This means that there is no bank or government control or prerequisites to be able to own or transfer a bitcoin. The symbol for bitcoin looks like ⃝ (different from the logo) or BTC just as we have USD for US dollars.

Bitcoin is a crypto currency, and crypto currencies have been around since 1980s, faced majorly with a problem called the "double spend." All of the prior digital currencies or crypto-currencies have had the problem where somebody spends a unit of that currency and difficult to tell if it is already being spent. That is the biggest problem that bitcoin have solved and it has gained so much popularity. The way it does this is through its distributed peer-to-peer network, which works kind of like torrents.

Someone apparently named Satoshi Nakamoto issued the first bitcoin in 2009, believed to be a pen name meaning nobody really knows who started bitcoin.

Therefore, there will actually only ever be 21 million bitcoins in circulation. In 2009, we had the first bitcoins released, and there is a predetermined amount of bitcoins that is released every 10minutes (we will talk about how that works in our next lesson). However, just know that over years, this will continue to happen until the year 2041.

Bitcoin is divisible down to the eight decimal place (.00000001) just like the US dollars divisible to a "penny" or two decimal place (.01). You can almost infinitely break down bitcoin to a very small amount.

The bitcoin protocol (the bitcoin network, or the way the bitcoin operates) have no central location of its governance by any specific country is very difficult and expensive to hack. Some say, "to hack the bitcoin network for 10minutes will cost around half a billion dollars". Therefore, there is a lot of trust and a lot of vetting of the protocol in the network has happened over the past few years.

It is controlled by the consensus of market participation. Again, no one government, no one person or no one group actually controls the bitcoin network, which is why it is gaining so much popularity.

The importance of Bitcoin

After all said and done, the question is why is bitcoin so important? Why am I teaching you about bitcoin? There are some aspects of crypto currencies that I think show huge prospects to really changing the world.

- Let us look at this first fact that out of 7+ billion people that live on the planet earth, about 6.5 billion people don't have access to basic financial banking services like checking accounts, or credit cards. In the US alone, we estimated that about 18% of people do not have access to these basic financial services. It (bitcoin) makes it very easy for anybody without government permission or control to have access to virtual banking. I think that is going to change the world.
- The second fact that we will look out here is, since the 2008 financial crisis, fiat currencies like the US dollars (if you are not familiar what fiat currencies are; it's a currency that is backed by nothing but the trust that people have in the

government) have failed. Back in the 70's, everyone was in the gold standard, and next we were taken off the standard. Now, the USD is no longer tied to anything. For example, I have kept one hundred genuine Zimbabwean dollars as a kind of reminder what can happen when government got off control by printing too much money. In the span of less than 2years, the Zimbabwe government essentially devalued their currency to nothing. In addition, there is a lot of speculation that some of the major world's fiat currencies are going in that same direction and this is somewhat scary because tight now the USD is the world's reserve currency and the government is just printing it like nobody's business. Therefore, the way bitcoin handles this problem is that there is a predetermined set amount of bitcoins to be released over the years. What that does is that it is inherently designed to be deflationary and really control inflation.

- The third kind of major problem that bitcoin really handles is the fact that "cross currency purchases" and "transfers across boundaries" are expensive and have a lot of friction (a lot of government "red-tape"). It will costs a lot of money to move millions of dollars, but with bitcoin it is very inexpensive and there are stories were people move millions and millions of dollars for just a few penny.

Money

Before we talk about the working principles of bitcoin, let us look at what is money.

Money is simply any means of exchanging goods and services. Recent history reviews fiat currencies (like USD) and gold as widely accepted forms of money. Primarily, four properties that define what money is are as follows.

1. It needs to be divisible (broken down into different parts or sizes or small amounts). That is why the dollars can be broken into two decimal places (a penny). Gold can also be broken down (you can have a ball, ounce)
2. It needs to be durable. That is, it needs to be able to stand the test of time. Therefore, if you have a ball of gold on your desk, our theory is that it is not just going to evaporate into thin air. Even one hundred trillion dollars is not likely to evaporate.
3. It needs to be fungible. Like commodity, one US dollars is equal to the value

another one US dollars. They are interchangeable kind of like on the futures market were people trade ounces, coffees, oil, gold etc. whose each unit is equal to another unit. They all are equal in value.
4. It needs to be verifiable. You need weigh and verify if it is real and not counterfeit

Therefore, I believe with this few points you can differentiate between "money" and the present day "fiat currency"

Lesson Two

Blockchain Technology

Blockchains are incredibly popular nowadays. What is a blockchain? How do they work? What problems do they solve? Moreover, how can they be used?

As the name indicates, a blockchain is a chain of blocks that contains information. This technique was originally described in 1991 by a group of researchers, and was originally intended to timestamp digital documents so that it is not possible to backdate them or to temper with them (almost like a note-read). However, it went by mostly unused until

Satoshi Nakamoto adopted it in 2009 to create a digital crypto currency, bitcoin.

Blockchain is a distributed ledger that is completely open to anyone. They have interesting properties. Once data have been recorded inside the blockchain, it becomes very difficult to change it.

How does that work? Well, let us take a closer look at a block; each block contains some data, hash of the block, and hash of the previous block.

The data that is stored inside the block depends on the type of the blockchain. The bitcoin blockchain for example stores the details about the transaction here such as the sender, the receiver, and the amount of coins.

A block also has a hash. You can compare a hash to be a fingerprint. It identifies a block and all of its contents and it is always unique just as a fingerprint. Once a block is created, its block is being calculated. Changing something inside the block will cause the hash to change. In other words, hashes are very useful when you want to detect changes to blocks. If the fingerprint of a block changes, it no longer exists in block

Hash of the previous block is the third element inside a block. This effectively creates a chain of blocks, and it is this technique that makes the blockchain secure. For example, if we have a chain of three blocks, each of them has a hash and a hash of the previous block. Block number three points to block number two, and number two points to number one. The first block is not so special, it cannot point to previous block because it is the first one (we call it **genesis block**). Now if you temper with the second block, it causes the hash of the block to change as well, in turn, that will make block three and all following blocks invalid because they no longer store a valid hash of the previous block. Therefore, changing a single block will make all following blocks invalid.'

Using hashes is not enough to prevent tempering. Computers are very fast and can calculate hundreds of thousands of hashes per second. You can effectively temper with a block and recalculate all the hashes of other blocks to make your blockchain valid again.

To mitigate this, blockchain has something called "Proof-of-work." A mechanism slows down the creation of new blocks. In bitcoins case, it takes about ten minutes to calculate the required proof of work and add a new block to the chain. This mechanism makes it very hard to tamper with the blocks, because if you tamper with one block you need to recalculate the proof-of-work for all the following blocks

Therefore, the security of a blockchain comes from its creative views of hashing and the proof-of-work mechanism. However, there is one more way that blockchain secure itself and that is by being distributed. Instead of using a central entity to manage chain, blockchain uses a peer-to-peer network and everyone is allowed to join. When someone joins this network, he gets a full copy of the blockchain. The nodes can use this to verify that everything is in order.

What happens when someone creates a new block?

The block is sent to everyone on the network, each that verifies the block to make sure that it has not been tampered with. In addition, if everything checks out, each node adds this block to their own blockchain. All the nodes in this network creates "consensus" – they agree about what blocks are valid. Nevertheless, other nodes in the network will reject blocks that are tampered with. Therefore, to successfully tamper with a blockchain, you need to tamper with all the blocks in the chain, redo the proof-of-work for each block and take control of more than fifty percent of the peer-to-peer network. Only then will everyone else accept your tampered block. Therefore, this is almost impossible to do

Blockchains are also constantly evolving. One of the most recent developments is the creation of what we call the "smart contract." These contracts are simple programs that are stored on the blockchain used in the automatic exchange of coins based on certain conditions. The creation of blockchain technology picks many peoples interests. Soon others will realize that this technology is useful in other things like

- Storing medical records
- Creating a digital notary (E-notary)
- Collection of taxes etc.

Now, you know what a blockchain is, how it works at the basic level, and what problem it solves.

Blockchain limitations

To every advantage, there is always a disadvantage. Therefore, there are also treacherous passes in any technological revolution. Some persons in the blockchain industry have pointed out that blockchain has become overhyped, when, in reality, the technology has limitations and inappropriate for many digital interactions. However, through research and development, success and failure, and trial & error, we have being able to learn the current issues and limitations of blockchain as discussed below.

Complexity: Blockchain technology involves an entirely new vocabulary. It has made cryptography more mainstream, but the highly specialized industry is chock-full of jargon. Thankfully, several efforts at providing glossaries and indexes are thorough and easy to understand.

Network size: Blockchains (like all other distributed systems) are not so much resistant to bad actors as they are "anti-fragile" – that is to say, they respond to attacks and grow stronger. However, this requires a large network of users. If a blockchain is not a robust network with a widely distributed grid of nodes, it becomes more difficult to reap the full benefit.

There is some discussion and debate about whether this as a fatal flaw for some permissioned blockchain projects.

Transaction costs, network speed: Bitcoin currently has notable transaction costs after being glorified as 'near free' for the first few years of its existence.

As of late 2016, it can only process about seven transactions per second and each transaction costs about $0.20 and can only store 80 bytes of data.

There is also the politically charged aspect of using the bitcoin blockchain, not for transactions, but as a store of information. This is the question of "bloating" and often frowned upon because it forces miners to perpetually reprocess and rerecord the information.

Politics: Because blockchain protocols offer an opportunity to digitize governance models, and miners are essentially forming another type of incentivized governance model, there have been many opportunities for public disagreements between different sectors of the community.

This disagreement are a notable feature of the blockchain industry and is expressed most clearly around the question or event of "forking" a blockchain, a process that involves updating the blockchain protocol when majorities of a Blockchains' users have agreed to it. These debates can be very technical, and sometimes heated, but informative to those interested in the mixture of democracy, consensus, and new opportunities for governance experimentation that blockchain technology is opening up.

Human error: If we use blockchain as a database, then the information going into the database needs to be of very high quality. In the first place, an event needs to be recorded accurately because the data stored on a blockchain is not inherently trustworthy. The phrase "garbage-in, garbage-out" holds true in a blockchain system of record, just as with a centralized database.

Unavoidable security flaw: Bitcoins and other Blockchains has one notable security flaw in; if more than half of the computers working as nodes to service the network tell a lie, the lie will automatically become the truth. This we call a "fifty-one percent attack" and highlighted by Satoshi Nakamoto during the launch of bitcoin.

For this reason, the community, ensuring no one unknowingly gains such network influence, monitors bitcoin mining pools closely.

Lesson Three
Bitcoin Value

Let us look at the ways we can derive value from bitcoin.

- It is limited and scarce (like gold). On planet earth, there is only a set amount of gold just like there is a limited amount of bitcoins. There will be only 21-million bitcoins that are ever mined, just the way you can only mine a certain amount of gold
- It is decentralized; there is no central government
- There is a peer-to-peer network (like torrents)

- It can be anonymous. Though there are awesome areas for improvements when it comes to this anonymous nature of crypto-currencies, but for the most part, it is anonymous.
- It is also transparent, meaning the code and the structure of how the bitcoin crypto-currency network and protocol exists is transparent. Anybody can go, evaluate, and look at how the code works. Because it is being vetted by people much smarter than you are and for over five years, make it trust worthy. People place their trust in the bitcoin protocol even more so than they are putting their trust in their own government, which is very interesting and the reason why the whole crypto-currency moment could really change the way that world leaders, governments, and people look at money.

- It is also very easy to buy and sell. We will talk about how bitcoin works and it is so easy just to move bitcoins among/between two people.
- There is extremely low transaction fees
- It is irreversible. So merchants love it, there are no charge backs and none of the problems you have when it comes to taking credit cards

It is important to keep in mind that bitcoin is not backed by anything tangible. Just like fiat currencies, it is not on the gold standard neither is it on anything except the trust that people have in the bitcoin system

The real value of bitcoins is determine by what people are willing to pay for it, which is why we have seen the price of bitcoin go up so much over the past couple of years because the demand has increased.

People place value in the following four aspects of bitcoin

- Lack of government control/manipulation
- Protection from inflation
- Trust in the bitcoin protocol where it will cost a half a billion dollars just to fall the system for about 10 minutes only.
- Anonymous nature

Working principle of bitcoins

How does bitcoin really work? It is very simple

- Let us say you take some money, somebody gives you cash or writes you a check, and you take it to a bank and you deposit it in your bank account. Well bitcoins kind of works like this

- When somebody gives you bitcoin, it (bitcoin) is stored in a public ledger. Everybody has access to this ledger from the very beginning in 2009. This forms the storehouse for all transactions.
- Sending and receiving bitcoins is as easy as sending an email. It is really fast and simple to do.
- Your coins are actually stored in "wallets."

There are a few different kinds of wallets.

- o You can store bitcoins in your local hard drive wallets, so there your coins actually live on your computer
- o You can have paper wallets were you will physically write down the codes associated onto your bitcoin and keep it off of the network
- o It can be hosted online. There are companies that are actually providing

hosted wallets were you could access your coin from anywhere in the world. That is were the security risk comes in.

With bitcoins, there is actually two parts to your bitcoin account

1. Public key; this is kind of like your account number or your email address. It consists of about 27-34 alphanumeric characters (it would look something like 172Exighk1qsMNdr124Yhd9855ggbHG) around 30 characters. This is the account number that you actually give out to anybody who wants to send you bitcoin. So, for example I wanted to send you five bitcoins, you give me your public key, I will type that in and shoot you over the bitcoins.
2. Private key; this is where the protection comes in. It is kind of like the password. For whenever you do online banking,

you need to know your password to login to your online banks, right. It is somewhat similar with private key, which is the password you need to access your bitcoins in the account or in that public ledger. It sounds complicate but it really is simple.

Lesson Four

How to acquire Bitcoins

There is actually three ways to acquire bitcoins.

1. Buy bitcoin from a person: You can go to anybody willing to sell and say, "Rob, I want to buy a bitcoin, you both look at the price of price of bitcoins, you give him dollars, and he gives you bitcoin. That is simple, or you can go to an exchange. There are websites like Coinbase, Coinomi, and Bitstamp and so on. This is where people meet to buy and sell from each other. Kind of like a stock market, right? Oh, yes!

2. You can batter: You can basically provide products or services in exchange for bitcoins
3. Mine for bitcoin: This is where bitcoin where released every ten minutes. There are miners out there who naturally mine for these bitcoins. It works kind of like a lottery system where the more, the more CPU power that you have and the more that you mine, the better the odds of getting these bitcoins free. You can do that by swing software on your computer. We will talk more on this in one of our lessons. So, stay put.

How to make profit with bitcoin

The question is how can you profit with bitcoin?

✓ Mine, and then sell: When you mine bitcoins, obviously, you get bitcoins free which you can in turn sell for whatever the market value is. Now, one thing to note is that it is becoming difficult. The more competition there is, the more computing power it takes to actually mine for these bitcoins, the more cost is associated – the more hardware you have to buy, the electricity you have to pay for. Therefore, before you say look, I just want to start mining bitcoins, you really have to do cost analysis to figure out if it is going to profit you.

- ✓ Invest or trade: This happens to be most traders' favorite way of making profit from bitcoins. You must heard around "hey! Look this bitcoin is a bubble." Mind you, there is a lot speculation out there; the prices have increased dramatically over the past couple of years. Therefore, we will talk about your options here. There are two options to this.

- o Buy & hold: I think the whole buy and hold mentality is risky. Anytime you say, "Honey, tonight I heard on sixty minutes that bitcoin is the new thing and it can take over the dollars, let us just go ahead, and buy at whatever the market price is right now. Ehm... That is a very risky strategy.
- o Short term trading: this happens to be another favorite method. This is what I do for over a decade now.

✓ Offer discounts in products & services for payment in bitcoins: This option is suitable for merchants (if you sell products or provides services). What many people do is that they offer discounts to people who want to pay in bitcoin. For example, if I am somebody who sells cups and decides, "Okay the value of the cup is one dollar. Well I know that if I expect the price of bitcoin to go up the next few years because of limited supply, then I can actually take a discount and sell it at a rate of fifty cents to those willing to pay in bitcoins. Therefore, if I accept that, it is a discount and that is what many people are doing. Recently, people have being purchasing houses, cars and others with bitcoins. In addition, recently many big merchants online have started accepting bitcoins making this period the most exciting time in history, and you are advised to be a part of this crypto currency movement.

Lesson Five

Bitcoin speculations

So, let us talk a little bit about bitcoins speculations.

1. Recently bitcoin have increased in value over one thousand percent for the past couple of years
2. Though the rise in price, we have also seen many crashes of over fifty percent or more. However, that is something to keep in mind.
3. In addition, as at the time of this publication, it is interesting to say that despite all the aforementioned speculations, bitcoin have recovered after each crash.

There many people speculating and saying "oh bitcoin is a big bubble, don't chase it." This I agree and as a professional trader, I am a huge proponent of not chasing what the herd is doing. We saw this in the housing bubble of the early 2000's. Even in a couple of years ago in 2011, we saw that with a gold bubble. People flock into an asset on investment vehicle and that drives prices up. Kind of like "too late maniac" if you have heard of that. Nevertheless, the idea is to understand if you are going to invest on something that has a long-term value.

4. There is a big question, which I think will determine if bitcoin is actually just a bubble, or a fact, which I do not think it is. "Will bitcoin become widely accepted as a form of payment and a store of value?" In other words, will the mass majority – people in the world – use bitcoin as a means of exchange over

other currencies (fiat currencies like the US dollars). Will they see value in it? Will they use it as a store of value the way they look at gold? If that remains true in the near future, I think the prices of bitcoin will stay valuable.

Speculation tips

Let me give you some advice when it comes to speculations because this is what I do.

1. Do not chase emotional buying: This is why so many people lose money in virtually every market (stock market, futures market, housing market, and now the bitcoin market). It has to do with when people chase emotional rises in price. Making money in the market is all anticipation, and understanding human psychology.

2. Do the opposite of the herd: This is what I always like to do. When everybody is panicking, I will like to look for opportunities to buy. When everybody is having bullish exuberance that tends to help in driving the prices of the market up, I get skeptical and look for reasons to sell. There is an old cliché quote by Warren Buffett that says, "When people are scared, be greedy, and when people are greedy, be scared." I think this applies to every market and especially the bitcoin.
3. Consider the risks and your goals. This is because bitcoin is just an experiment. It is really the first successful crypto currency, and right now, there are over one hundred alternative crypto currencies (alt-coins). No one knows if within a long time bitcoins is going to be

a kind of a merge or revolve. You have to put that in mind.

In addition, I would not recommend on training or investing in bitcoin with money you could not afford to lose, because there are some significant risks with bitcoin that we are going to talk about soon.

4. Is day (short term) trading really riskier than the "buy and hold" mentality? This is the last question am going to pose here. My thesis is, "I want to have predefined trades that am looking for that I think have a high probability of success, that I can control my risk and really predetermine where my profit targets are and were my risks are, were I will stop out and take a loss. I think approaching the market from a very mechanical and mathematical approach is a better way to control risk than say,

"Honey, I just want to buy in the stock market, bitcoin market and hope it grows for a few years." If you live through the financial crisis of 2008, you would probably experience that pain. I know a lot of people that were very bullish in the market in 2007, you had some idiots on CNBC telling people "the market is going great, everybody needs to buy, it is all time high." Few months later, the markets were down and people sold their retirements account because they saw it fall by fifty percent. They panicked, they thought the American economy was going shake, they sold out at the bottom and missed the four-year boom market that happened after that.

Therefore, it is my job here as a training educator to help people break away from the herd mentality and to see things from what they really are.

Lesson Six

Risks of Using the Bitcoins

Let us talk about the risks/dangers of bitcoins

- The biggest risk is "bugs in the code or problems with the bitcoin protocol that lead to a complete lack of confidence in bitcoin. Something that could happen if never been hacked or if people ever said, "Look ,we cannot trust the bitcoin protocol," you have a flight from that currency and see it crash to almost zero. I think that is a very real risk, but the probability of that happening is very low. That is why over-all am bullish in bitcoin, and I actually believed that bitcoin or at least crypto currencies is going to change the world someday.

- Government or political interventions
- Competing crypto currencies: There are over a hundred alternative coins right now. So if one of those coins solves a problem (big enough) that bitcoin does not right now, and then everybody could transfer into that coin. Though that's yet to be seen and be very skeptical of anybody who says that they knows what is going to happen with bitcoins. Anybody who owns many bitcoins is probably bullish on bitcoin and wants to see it succeed. Anybody who is a hater or feels they are late to the game or does not quite understand it; they might be neigh sellers without truly understanding the moment that is happening right now.

Also,

How do I keep my Bitcoin safe?

Recognizing frauds to reduce the risks:
Successful criminals operate on the fringes of technological innovation and take advantage of people who are still learning. They stay ahead of law enforcement agencies and regulation. Therefore, as with any new technology, there are risks associated with digital currencies. Understand the risks and ensure that you have the tools to protect yourself and your money.

Phishing attacks
Owning digital currency makes you more vulnerable to cybercrime. Ensure you hook up with the right exchanges in order to keep your Bitcoin safe (security). Only you can keep your passwords safe. 'Phishing' is an attack whereby criminals use legitimate-looking fake websites to trick you into entering your

password/details. They use your password to access your account.

Different types of phishing attacks

- Phishing websites: Fraudsters create fake versions of websites to try to get you to enter login details. Beware of clicking through from fake Google ads. Before entering any of your details, check the website address carefully to make sure you are at the correct URL.
- Email phishing: Fraudsters will send legitimate-looking emails in an attempt to convince you to share login details. Check the sender email and make sure the website to which they direct you to have the correct address.
- Spear phishing. Fraudsters try to gain information about a specific individual. If they know you have digital currency, they may even impersonate digital

currency company employees to gain your trust. These impersonators may contact you by phone or email.

You might think you will be able to spot traps and avoid them. However, ask yourself this, are you one hundred percent confident in every link you have ever clicked? Are you willing to bet all your Bitcoin on that?

Safety measures includes the following
- Always check your browser address bar to make sure you are visiting the correct website address and not a fake site
- Use two-factor authentication on all your email addresses and your Bitcoin wallets
- Always use a password manager program
- If you are using a Gmail account, do a quick security check

Investment frauds: Because the digital currency space is relatively young, there are investment frauds trying to part you from your money. Frauds come in all shapes and sizes but with a little practice, you can easily spot and avoid them.

Cloud mining frauds: Ninety-nine percent of cloud mining operations are suspicious. Legitimate Bitcoin miners will tell you that the profit margins on mining are razor thin.
There is nobody out there mining Bitcoin, making ten percent, twenty percent, and thirty percent per month as these frauds are promising. Avoid these at all costs.

Multi-level marketing frauds: If the company is punting its referral program harder than its product, it is probably a fraud.

Chances are they are paying existing investors with new investors' deposits. Eventually the music stops and they disappear, leaving everybody out of pocket, and only then do victims realize they actually have no idea to whom they sent their money.

Bitcoin "doublers" or high yield investment programs (Ponzi schemes): These fraudsters convince you that they have found a special or secret method to making incredible returns. Whether it is trading on your behalf, or exploiting technical aspects of digital currency. In reality, they have not found anything - if they had, they would not need your investment. Their only skill is conning you. Move along, swiftly.

How to spot a fraud/scam

Make sure you do some research before investing in something. If the returns thy promise sound too good to be true, then it is probably a fraud. Also, check out the bad list at www.badbitcoin.org. If it is listed here, it means it is definitely suspicious and almost certainly a fraud.

Volatile markets

Although this is not related to criminal activity, but it is important to be aware that Bitcoin and other digital currencies are exceptionally volatile. Price fluctuations can be violent at times and it is important that you do not risk inappropriate amounts of money (more than you can afford to lose). Keep in mind that during violent market movements, misinformation is in most cases spread in the news, and digital currency service providers may experience service disruptions. You may not always be able to sell your digital currency at a moment's notice.

So just, take time to educate yourself and look at both sides equally.

Lesson Seven

Bitcoin wallets

Welcome back, in this lesson we will be talking about bitcoin wallets

The question is "what really is a bitcoin wallet? A bitcoin wallet is a way to store your bitcoins either virtually or physically,

Types of wallets

There is only four different type of wallets

1. Software that you actually install in your computer and lives on your hardware
2. Mobile; you can have an iPhone or droid, basically have an app or you can manage your bitcoin from there

3. Hosted online; you can also host them with a company online
4. Paper; have physical paper wallets

To know more about the basic information you can visit www.bitcoin.org website and you will see the different options to acquaint yourself. However, they do not talk about paper wallet in there, but we will get to that soon.

Software wallets: The nice thing about software wallet is that you have complete control and anonymity – it is anonymous. You do not have information floating around online. It has the following characteristics

- It is physically stored on your hard drive. Meaning it does not have to be connected to the internet.
- It is important you make sure to back up your physical wallets because when you do not have it backed up any were, and

your computer dies, or something/someone comes in and steals your computer, all will be lost. You might have heard a story of someone who lost about six million dollars' worth of bitcoin. Because he forgot that he had a bunch of bitcoin on his computer threw it away and had to go through thousand tons worth of trash to try to find his computer. However, I do not know if he finally found it. In either ways, if you want to make sure you have a software wallet better back it up.
- One of the most popular wallets for your computer is Bitcoin-Qt

Cloud Hosted: This is the second option that you have. The benefit here is that

- You can access your bitcoin from anywhere around the world with a high-speed internet connection.
- Online wallets with this websites that you can use the wallets can act, as exchanges were you could actually buy and sell. They do not just hoard your coins. For example, the Bitcoin-Qt is not an exchange; it is just a software program.

Some of the risks of cloud-hosted wallets are

- Hackers: There have been stories of some of the exchanges and some of the online wallets that have actually been hacked. So were I have complete confidence in the security of the protocol (bitcoin network) is that it cannot be hacked and the only thing that can be

hacked is the online websites that holds your information.
- Company default: When an exchange or company goes out of business, then you know in theory that your bitcoin has gone into thin air.
- Not anonymous: with a lot of these exchanges and online wallets, you have to verify your information and in a lot of cases want some really personal information (stuff)

Examples of these cloud-hosted websites are like the blockchain.info, coinbase.com etc.

Mobile Wallets: From my list, this happens to be the third option. Again, there is third party risk here. They are apps for droid or iPhone. You can go to blockchain.info to educate yourself more on some other information about wallets.

Paper Wallets: This is the final type of wallet am going to talk about. This is really the safest way to store bitcoin if you take care of it. Now, if you take your bitcoin offline into a physical paper and then loose the paper, it is kind of like having a gold delivered to your house and later lost. You can buy gold and have it stored somewhere else, or you can buy gold and actually hold it somewhere in your house.

What you do here is to generate a public and private key from your browser or you can download the generator and actually print out physical bitcoins. Well, it does not matter if its hand written or printed on official real glossy paper. The only thing that matter is the public and private key

Lesson Eight

Bitcoin exchanges

At this stage, we are going to be talking about bitcoin exchanges. In other words, "how to buy and sell bitcoins."

How to buy & sell bitcoins

Talking about how to buy and sell bitcoins, there is actually a couple of options.

1. **Peer-to-peer:** this is simply person-to-person. You can come to me or anyone else and say, "Hi, I want to buy bitcoins," we look at the price and I say "great," give me your address (public key), I send you your bitcoin, you get me cash and we are good to go.
    - Digital or physical: if you have a paper wallet with a private and give me cash,

gold, cars (depending on our terms), I can get you your bitcoins.

- Localbitcoins.com: it is kind of like an eBay. It deals with one buyer, and one seller, which I do not really think is the most efficient way and you may probably overpay if you do that.

2. **Exchange:** this is the second option which can be;
- A virtual meeting place for people to buy and sell at an agreed market price, just like the way the stock market works. It is an exchange where you have a ton of people who is going to buy and a ton of people ready to sell, meaning everybody is buying and selling. Through that, you have what we call "price discovery" – you find out what the true market value is – based on demand and supply. It

makes really efficient and just good for all market participant

Working Principle of Exchanges

- What the exchanges do is that they provide efficient environment for people to buy and sell crypto-currencies. This is not just for bitcoins; you also have Litecoin exchanges and other alternative coin. Most of those have their own exchange. Bitcoin have the most market volume, biggest market cap, most value out there, which is why we focused on bitcoin.
- The way that this works is that the website or the exchange takes a percentage of the trade. Anyway, usually from a tenth to as high as one percent, so it can be expensive if you are not careful. You really need to make sure

that you are trading with the right exchanges.
- The way that you get started is that you basically need to sign with an exchange to start trading
- Some of them do require verification especially if you are going to link a bank account or moving bitcoins into fiat currencies.

Popular exchanges

Let us talk about some of the popular exchanges. At the time of this publication there are about 4-5 exchanges that we will go through and we are going to talk about each one. However, just to know that over next couple of years this could change because bitcoin again is really a new environment. I see some issues in some of the exchanges and see many opportunities for improvements.

Therefore, we have to see how this evolves over the next few months and years.

1. **Coinbase:** this is the first we are going to talk about, and if you are in the US, I think this is a great way to get started. It is technically an exchange, but I do not think it is the best place to buy and sell (trade) because their fees are very high. The nice thing about this platform is that if you are in the states, you can link it with your bank account and buy/sell bitcoin quickly. In our next lesson, I am going to teach you how to sign up with this and get your first bitcoins.
2. **Bitstamp:** This is the second option I really like. Bitstamp looks like BTC-e; they have the same functionalities.
3. **BTC**-e
4. **MtGOX:** This is an overseas account especially for those from the States that is overseas. Though am not a fan of

MtGox, am just speculating here, but I think they have sovereign issue. I do not know how legitimate they really are. Time will not permit to go into details on that.

5. **Bitfinex:** This is the final one and I really enjoy trading though. I actually saw through – so you can make money buying long, buying low and selling high – this one. You can also make money if the price of bitcoin goes down. We call this "shorting" – you sell first and buyback at a lower price.

Now, let us take a brief walk.

At Bitstamp, you can buy and sell. They have their own market price. In addition, BTC-e, very similar has its own market price too. At the time of this publication, Bitstamp and BTC-e have relative similar prices while MtGox because of their liquidity issues you will notice that the price tends to be a lot higher than the other markets. Therefore, I do not really look at MtGox as a true representation of the bitcoin value. Finally, Bitfinex, while it is a great one were you can actually lend bitcoins to people that wants to trade on margin or want to short; because to short mean actually borrow bitcoins. We will talk about that in one of our lessons coming up shortly. At bitcoinaverage.com, you get a feel from the market cap and the average market price.

Bitcoin price

The price of bitcoin is simply whatever two people agree to buy/sell bitcoins. So you can go to someone down the streets and say "look I will pay you five bucks for a bitcoin," and if he is stupid, he will say "okay cool," give me five bucks and here is your bitcoins. Then you can go to the market and sell it for whatever the market price is.

However, the exchanges remove the guessing, they remove the friction of buying and selling. It is advisable you use bitcoinaverage website to determine the average market price. For clarity, you can use bitcoinwisdom.com (for charts and predictions) or tradingview.com.

How to protect private keys

It is very important to store your Bitcoins safely. Unlike other types of money that the banks have control over, with Bitcoin you have many more options on how to store and control your money.

Do you remember you need your private key to move your Bitcoin? Well that is literally the key to storing it. Whoever has the key controls the Bitcoin. These keys can be in either digital or even in physical format (i.e. written down on a piece of paper).

How then can you store it? You can decide to leave the key in your pocket, but that is not too secure. You can put it in a safe – that is a lot better. Nevertheless, someone can still break into your house (safe) and steal it. Given you want to use your Bitcoin regularly; one might also want to put some or all of it in a digital version on your phone so you can access it easier. The only problem now is that if you lose your phone it means you will also lose your key, and there is no way to get it back.

That is why companies like Luno, Bitfinex, Bitstamp, and others exist - not just to make it easier to buy/sell and use Bitcoin, but also to store it securely. They do this by taking your private keys and storing them in a physical bank vault with access controls like fingerprint and retina scans. In fact, it is not just one vault; it is a number of vaults across many continents. And we build it in a way that you have to access the keys from multiple vaults and put them together to actually be able to extract the Bitcoin, similar to the old movies where nuclear submarines need 3-5 'launch codes' from different generals to be able to launch nuclear weapons. This is called 'multisig' (multiple signatures required).

Bitcoin is very safe when it is stored like this, but there is one potential weak link: you need to trust the people storing the keys on your behalf. Many reputable companies like Luno, Bitfinex, that you can rely on, but also many others either do not store it properly or might pretend to store it and then misappropriate it. The great thing about Bitcoin is that, unlike old money you have the choice whether to store it yourself in physical or digital format, or whether you rely on someone else to safeguard it for you, or even a combination of all of these

The way Bitcoin is often stored is also one of the biggest ironies of Bitcoin being the world's global currency that was designed to be used online, is in most cases stored 'offline', in physical bank vaults and detached from the internet. Who would have thought!

Lesson Nine
Coinbase

What is Coinbase? Coinbase is an online-hosted wallet and it is an American based company out of San Francisco. At the time of this publication, they have more than six hundred and fifty thousand accounts; over sixteen thousand merchants are actually using Coinbase to accept payments. They integrate with US banks. For example, you can plug your checking accounts into Coinbase and buy bitcoins relatively quickly.

How to set up Coinbase

Go to www.coinbase.com and sign up for an account. Fund it with at least one hundred US dollars and Coinbase will give you ten dollars free of bitcoin. That is cool, right

Register for an account. There are two verification levels and I will teach you in a short while. I wish everything is instantaneous and you can just buy as many bitcoins you want overnight quickly. However, there is a little bit of a process that you go through. It is worth doing sooner than later. That way you are not kicking yourself if bitcoin prices go up or if you mess with a real profitable trade. So just, go ahead and do it while you can.

- After you have made your verification, what you will do is to **"activate the ability to buy bitcoin instantly."** Now, get this, when you have finished the process of **sign-up,** you will notice that there are actually two verification levels;

In level 1: This is where you are verify your email address (click the link with the confirmation email). It is easy, right

Next, you verify your phone number. This is important because, it really add kind of a second level security.

Thirdly, you link a bank account. Now, some people do not want to put all their information through these exchanges and they just want to buy peer to peer, though that is okay too. This is for somebody that wants to be a trader of bitcoin, or if you want to have an instant access to the market.

I feel fine with Coinbase and a lot of other exchanges, but again they all going to ask for a personal information for you to be able to use this information. That is level one, and what this level will get you is a daily buy limit of fifty bitcoins. It actually takes about four days for the bitcoins to arrive when you make your first purchase. It is not as if you can buy/sell right away on your first transaction. I recommend that you go ahead and do level one as quickly as possible, so that you get the clock ticking.

After thirty days, you will be able eligible for level two. However, you do have to wait for thirty days after you have bought your first bitcoins. So go ahead and link it all up. Buy just a little amount of bitcoin to get yourself started. On level one, I believe you will get 0.1btc instant buy, so after you do your first purchase, you can buy all of it very quickly. They do this for security reasons.

In level two, after you have complete a purchase and wait for at least thirty days like I mentioned, you can verify your identity by sending in some information. Some of these exchanges want two things; they want 1-ID or proof of who you are and a proof of residence (kind of like a utility bill or something). This level will give you up to about ten bitcoins instant buy. You can buy and have in your account right away.

Therefore, I think Coinbase is really a good place where you can buy your first bitcoins, but it is not necessarily the best exchange for day trading. If you are going to be a trader, and you want to buy/sell for profit I recommend you use Bitstamp, BTC-e. Besides, if you want to short and make money as bitcoins comes down which I have actually made money from, I recommend you use Bitfinex. If you are outside the US, there are other alternatives like Luno, Cryptopia etc.

Lesson Ten
HOW TO MAKE MONEY-TRADING BITCOIN

No trader – be you a professional or an amateur – will dump/neglect this part. Besides this happens to be my favorite topic because making money while trading bitcoin is what I do as a professional trader. I have been doing this for over a decade now. However, before we dive in, please make sure you have understood all other lessons beforehand to be well acquainted with the working principle of the protocol. There is no short cut, because if you do not understand the basics I do not know how you can trade efficiently.

Trading: so now, let us go ahead and dive in. what is trading? Trading is where you buy and sell stuff and you keep the profit. That is kind of the real basic way to say it. Now, there is a couple of ways to do that.

- Go long: this is where you buy low, sell high and keep the difference. You can do that with stocks, futures, real estate, and now bitcoin. You can buy something at a dollar and sell it at ten dollars then keep the difference. What many people do not know is that they can actually make money as price of things comes down.
- Go short: You can actually sell first, though this might sound a little crazy because many have never heard of it. You can actually go short by selling first – sell high – and then buy back later at a lower price, then keep the difference. Therefore, you can make money as price of something goes up and as the price comes down.

Now you cannot short everything. I do not think you can short physical real estate, but you can short ETF (exchange trading fund), futures, bitcoin, stocks, and forex

- Arbitrage: this is where you buy at an exchange A and immediately sell some bitcoin at exchange B and keep the difference. Arbitrage is actually very difficult to do in the bitcoin market. The spreads (bid, ask spreads) are very big (meaning what you can buy and what you sell for). Specifically a lot of room there and the fees for bitcoin are quite high as well. In many cases, it does not make sense to do arbitrage. But what is a lot easier is what we call directional trading, where you buy low, sell high or sell high, and buy back lower.

Reasons to trade bitcoin

Let us talk about some of the benefits of trading bitcoin.

- It is very volatile meaning there are big swings in prices on the news. In addition, everybody is afraid of volatility, they keep saying "Oh! The market is so volatile right now, what do we do? When do we have a big swing here and a big swing there?" for day traders, that's where the money is made, that is where you can clean up and make a ton of money; because when things are boring and a kind of flat and steady, that's where it is kind of difficult to pull money of the market. What create this right now are many emotions in bitcoin. You have a lot of speculations, people just finding out about bitcoin and they are going, "oh my God, bitcoin is taking over the dollars, let me just put all my retirement into that," "oh bitcoin is

falling (panic) let me sell." Moreover, what that does is that it creates a big swing in the price.
- Right now, it is easy to predict because there is a lot of dumb money in the market. People are just throwing dollars "in" and "out" of the market creating big swings. Therefore, if you are a trader and understand human psychology, you can make a lot of money.

Things to consider

Now there are some things to consider before you get started.

- There is no regulated exchanges – no government/personal control. There is no oversight/watch-dog to take care of you if an exchange goes under the earth, they will try to screw you over. So you have to be conservative and be aware of the exchanges that you are trading through, because this a worldwide risk.

- There is big bid/ask spreads as mentioned earlier. If you want to buy a bitcoin and then sell it right away, there is spread there (for example, over here a group of people willing to buy bitcoin for six thousand dollars and another group wants to sell for six thousand one hundred dollars, that's a one hundred dollars spread). So if you are somebody who said "I want to buy, then buys at $6,100 from the seller. However, if you turn around and sell for $6,000 bid to the first buyer you lose 100-bucks.
- The fees right now in bitcoin are high. For example, anytime you have a new market the fees and commissions are always higher than they are after the market becomes established.

- It is best to trade for a minimum move of five percent in the price of bitcoins, (for example if bitcoin is for one thousand bucks, you want to see it move five percent, and I think that is fifty bucks). The reason why is because of the fees and spreads. If you are trying to trade to make a few pennies or couple of dollars, at the end of the day, you are not going to make any money because the fees and spreads will eat your life. The slippage too – if you try to buy with a market order, you can get a bad feel, and pay a lot higher than you really wanted to. The best thing to do in your trade is to look for potential moves. That is, the potential for bitcoin to move at least ten to twenty percent.

Choosing an exchange

Remember in one of our previous lessons we talked about choosing an exchange. However, let me reiterate some things.

- Coinbase is actually a great place to start buying your first bitcoins. However, it is better not to actively do bitcoin trades here because the fees are high. They are not really set up that way.
- The best exchanges for active trading known so far as at the time of this publication are Bitstamp, BTC-e, Bitfinex (good for shorting), and MtGOX. These are really the four kind of major ones. Over ninety-nine percent of the bitcoin market share traded is through these four exchanges. If you want to short, sign-up with Bitfinex, which I highly recommend because you make just as much money if not more on the downside than trying to buy. Everybody thinks they have to speculate

in just buy low and sell high; but that is not so, taking the downside is much more profitable.

Go through the headache of signing-up and verify your information, it will make your life easier.

Lesson Eleven

Bitcoin trading strategy

Here we are going to look at my bitcoin trading strategy, which happens to be the best secretes the world has ever known. Therefore, am going to give a thirty thousand foot overview of my strategy.

- Use technical analysis (look at charts, candlesticks, price bars and moving averages etc.) to help understand what the herd is doing. What the mass majority of people are thinking, believing and actions they are taking. Use it to deduce if people are panicking, there is exuberant bullishness, prices are going parabolic and shooting to the moon. Therefore, we can use technical analysis to qualify what is really happening. It is a visual representation of the action of all market participants.

- It is important to think like a contrarian, in other words, do the opposite of what the masses do. About ninety percent or more in every financial market lose money. Imagine if there are ten people in a room that are trading bitcoin, nine out of ten are probably going to lose money. Therefore, if you are smart, that is a good thing. That is a lot of dumb money in the market.
- When people are panicking in some cases, look for places to buy. Look for reasons to

buy when others are selling. You cannot just catch a falling knife like as the price is falling, there you go, "okay, the price of bitcoin is falling, am just going to buy." Believe me, that is not a strategy, I guess it is just kind of an idea.

- When people are scrambling to buy, look for places to sell. Everybody knows the old cliché of "buy low, sell high," but nobody actually does it. Everybody ends up doing the opposite because of fear and greed, which are really the two primary emotions that go on in the market. Therefore, understanding human psychology is going to be your best bet.

- Ride a trend if you can get in early meaning, do not chase height. It does not mean you cannot buy if the price of bitcoin is going up, but you need to think in terms of wholesale opportunity. For example, you own a bicycle shop and want to sell premium bikes to go for a thousand dollars. You are not going to buy at a thousand and hope to sell it at the same price/amount. You are going to think of how to get a bike at lower price and sell higher. Therefore, this kind of thinking is also applicable to the bitcoin market as well. That bitcoin is speculated to change the world (which I am part of) does not mean it is worth buying at any price. You have to be smart with risk management and have understanding of the human psychology.

Therefore, it is important to know the difference between short-term trading and longer-term investments. Don't just be one hundred percent bullish, understand what is happening in bitcoin, what the herd mentality is doing and you will end up being on the right side of the trade.

Notes:

CPSIA information can be obtained
at www.ICGtesting.com
Printed in the USA
BVHW031142210221
600726BV00025B/260